Dealing with Loneliness

Learn How to Deal with and Overcome Loneliness to Never Feel Alone Again

by Mary Jane Perruso

Table of Contents

Introduction

Do you think of yourself as persistently feeling lonely or alone? Often, people tend to shy away from categorizing themselves as "lonely", because it's perceived to be a sign of timidity, an inability to socialize, or an act of cowardice. Nobody wants to be categorized negatively like this, even in their own mind. But the fact still exists that loneliness is a very real state of being for millions of people. And to some degree, it's a perfectly normal and healthy feeling, as long as you are willing to take action and do something about it when it starts to bother you.

Although loneliness isn't a life threatening condition, have you ever observed the effects of it in your personal life? Were you able to control the automatic reactions of your body towards stress and your long moments of feeling so alone? Commonly, awareness of loneliness is the last thing that people want to acknowledge, and thus, its effects remain unnoticed and ignored – until you get to the point where they can no longer be ignored. But can you envision what your life might look like if you were able to instantly take action to address the loneliness instead of remaining in that state for extended periods of time? Since you're here reading this now, I think it's safe to assume you've already come to the conclusion that you often feel lonely, and you want to do something about it. Well good news: That's exactly what I'm going to help you with. Let's get started!

Chapter 1: What Loneliness Really Is

Loneliness is a perception that results from the reaction produced in response to environmental stimuli. Environmental stimuli are the external factors that you are exposed to. These stimuli may or may not cause a reaction, depending on your previous experiences.

The reaction is based on the cognition and interpretation of the person towards the stimulus. This triggers an emotion that brings sadness and isolation. Loneliness is only a concept of being alone and does not necessarily mean you're totally isolated.

Loneliness is most commonly classified under one of two categories:

1. *Loneliness that comes from hurt and pain.* This is typically as a result of relationship-breakups or marriage discord, loss of loved ones, achievement or expectation failures, or rejections. All these can lead a person to a partial or total isolation in order to cope with his feelings of loneliness, sadness, anxiety and depression.

People undergoing this type of loneliness don't know they are lonely because they concentrate more on the feeling and emotion brought on by the interpretation of the stimulus. It is the people around them who usually notice the changes in their behavior.

This kind of loneliness can lead to chronic loneliness that lasts longer without the person knowing it. If it remains unmanaged, it can cause unobserved, cumulative, adverse effects on the person's health. In this phase, affected persons usually need medical intervention such as psychotherapy or psychiatric treatment.

Psychotherapy is a kind of medical intervention mediated by a therapist. Sometimes, psychotherapy is also referred to as "talk therapy." It is typified by a "question and answer" portion using purposeful techniques in incorporating different ways to analyze the problem.

Upon the initiation and intervention of a therapist, the person is encouraged to talk in order to identify and acquire an insight into the root causes of his loneliness. This will help him cope, manage and overcome his problems to prevent unnecessary and unhealthy consequences including psychological disorders. Identification of the cause of loneliness is the primary basis for all therapies.

2. *Loneliness that emanates from isolation due to differences of faith and belief.* This type of loneliness can be quickly managed by the person's belief in a higher power or being. Hence, the loneliness takes on a new context. In addition, this type of isolation does not necessarily lead to loneliness. Being considered a pariah can lead to loneliness, but eventually, the person's faith will help him cope with his situation.

The difference between solitude and loneliness

Take note that solitude is different from loneliness. Solitude is enjoying being alone without feeling sad. You can be in solitude but happy and productive at the same time.

Doing things alone does not mean you are necessarily lonely. A person can be content and fulfilled from within and not feel sadness even without company. In fact, when you look at it positively, you can do various positive things when you're alone. You can work on your personal growth and devote quality time to yourself.

In other words, the interpretation of loneliness is based on your understanding and concept as a person in congruence with the environmental factors that you are facing.
Misinterpretation of being lonely can be harmful, especially if you don't do anything about it and it becomes chronic

loneliness. When this happens, your physical and mental processes will be altered, which is dangerous to your health. The worst scenario is that these negative effects can become irreversible.

Chapter 2: How Loneliness Affects the Brain

In a healthy state of mind, an individual can experience happiness, satisfaction, tranquility and peace of mind. However, when a threat presents itself such as, hurt, pain, and fear, the body has a natural way of reacting to these stimuli. Loneliness is highly associated with stress, anxiety and depression because these are categorized as reactions against environmental stimuli.

Many studies reveal that during times of loneliness and acute stress, stress hormones like epinephrine and adrenaline are relatively increased, while the cortisol level is prominently high during chronic stress and depression. These are the response hormones alerted in times of stress. These emotions create changes in the metabolic functions of the body, and in turn the body counterbalances the feelings and sensations received.

I am so stressed!

When you're stressed, hormones are released to prepare the body to negate the perceived threat or stimulus (physical, mental or emotional) coming from this external factor. The nervous system can detect all the possible stimuli from the environment and automatically responds towards averse emotion or perceived danger to the body.

The brain is stimulated when you're exposed to stressors, and thus discharges norepinephrine in the bloodstream. Norepinephrine is a neurotransmitter released from neurons, which stimulate the adrenal medulla of the kidney to release adrenaline.

The stress hormone adrenaline has many functions:

- Adrenaline gives your body a boost of energy by rapidly discharging glucose to the blood to contradict your feelings of being down. It also prepares your body with a "fight-or-flight response" when facing real or perceived dangerous situations. It gives an enormous strength "boost" to the body in case you want to face the enemy or run faster away from them.

- It inhibits other body processes like digestion and excretion, which is least needed in emergency instances to specifically allocate strength and energy to your other body parts, where it is needed the most. These are your muscles, skeletal tissues and brain.

- It increases your heart beat to pump more blood into your system, thus increasing your blood pressure. This is needed so that more blood can circulate in your body to make each of your organs work better and faster.

- It also enhances oxygen delivery to your brain. This will help you think faster and bolster your prompt decision-making skills.

These are all the initial reactions of your body to regain homeostasis and counteract your exposure to the stressor.

A prolonged bout of loneliness can lead to depression and chronic loneliness. In this instance, the hypothalamus of the brain releases the corticotropin-releasing hormone (CRH) that stimulates the pituitary gland which in turn releases adrenocorticotropic hormone (ACTH). ACTH is also known as corticotrophin.

What's Up, Cortisol?

ACTH goes into the bloodstream and is then transported to the kidneys, which will further stimulate the adrenal cortex to discharge cortisol.

Cortisol is the primary regulatory hormone secreted during stressful situations and depression to restore your body's proper homeostasis. The main regulatory function of cortisol is to inhibit the action of insulin, which will raise your blood sugar levels by increasing the metabolism of fats into energy. This process is known as gluconeogenesis. It provides a burst of energy and strength needed in emergency situations.

Cortisol also prepares your body for its "fight or flight responses." An elevated level of glucose will provide the needed strength if you want to fight or run.

When cortisol is released and reaches the required level to effectively deal with the stressor, your body has its own self-regulatory ability to shut down further production. The balance of cortisol in the body is then restored.

Your continuous exposure to stressors will trigger added generation of cortisol which can disable the proper function of the feedback loop mechanism. This can result in unceasing elevation of cortisol leading to harmful health effects.

Chapter 3: The Consequences of Prolonged Loneliness

Your persistent exposure to stressors can result in many adverse health conditions. Prolonged loneliness can result in depression. This, in turn, can lead to the following:

1. **A decrease in the capability of the immune system to control infection.**

   The destructive effect of cortisol on your immune system is due to the inhibition of the functions of some immune cells - primarily T cells - to recognize the presence of pathogens such as, bacteria, viruses or parasites in the body.

   Cortisol can mask the body's capability that is necessary for the identification of "non-self" antigen. This makes a person vulnerable to many diseases through depleted immune responses. People affected by chronic loneliness are highly susceptible to immunosuppression.

   Natural killer cells, which are essential in the destruction of cancer cells, are also obstructed. This will allow the proliferation of cancer cells that can invade the different organs to cause diseases. An increased level of cortisol can also block the capability of natural killer cells to detect the presence of cancer cells.

According to studies, women have the higher tendency to acquire cancer due to stressful situations, whether these are physical, mental or emotional.

2. Diabetes

Consistent elevation of glucose in your bloodstream due to persistent production of cortisol can result in diabetes, kidney failure, and eventually, vision impairment. Continuous involuntary suppression of the digestive process will consequently develop into problems related to overweight and obesity.

3. Coronary Heart Disease

Continuous exposure to stressors will increase your blood pressure which can cause nonstop exhaustion and strain to your heart. This can further lead to increased thickening of the walls of your arteries and decreased blood volume entering the heart. To compensate for the lower blood volume, the heart will pump more and work harder resulting in additional excessive pressure and trauma to the heart. This can further lead to many heart diseases.

It has also been observed in clinical studies that, during times of depression, there is an increase in blood clotting ability, which can cause heart attack and stroke.

4. Cognition Impairment

The normal level of cortisol has no adverse effects on the hippocampus. The hippocampus is a part of your brain where memory forming, processing, organizing and storage are performed. Many of the cortisol receptors are located in this part of the limbic system structure.

If excessive amounts of cortisol are stored in this part of the brain, atrophy and damages to the hippocampus can occur. This can result in concentration and memory loss, and impairment of the brain. Alzheimer's disease and senile dementia can emerge.

Some studies have shown that prolonged loneliness can also affect the structure of the brain. Because of the brain's ability to become accustomed and adapted to the environmental change, there is a probability that chronic loneliness will continually cause an anti-social attitude, even when the temporary isolation is over.

5. Premature Aging

Aside from the inhibition of digestive processes, growth and anti-aging hormones are also suppressed. The inhibition of the release of the anti-aging hormone prevents the development of new cells. This will result in persistently dry skin or slower wound healing due to the incapability of the cells to reinvigorate or re-grow. In addition, high cortisol brings interrupted sleep, which is significantly needed in the development of new cells. Insufficient rest makes you feel tired and fatigued all day, making you more stressed which also prevents your body from counteracting the aging process.

6. Infertility

In periods of loneliness, the function of your reproductive system is also impaired. Your immune, digestive and endocrine systems become dysfunctional, producing fewer hormones. Likewise, the decreased secretion of your sex hormones can lead to infertility in either male or female.

Because of the dramatic reduction of blood flow in the uterus, conception could become difficult in the chronic stress period - meaning conception might not happen anymore. That's why doctors advise de-stressing exercises to women who are having a hard time getting pregnant.

7. Psychosis

High levels of cortisol could also increase the release of dopamine. Dopamine is a chemical and neurotransmitter. As a signal transmitter between neurons or nerve cells, dopamine regulates and controls your movements and emotional responses to pleasant sensations.

Studies have shown that markedly reduced dopamine activity could lead to Parkinson's disease. Parkinson's disease is a neurodegenerative disease affecting movement. It is a nervous system disorder, which is gradual and progressive. The common signs are tremors, slurred speech, and slow or stiff movements.

Too much secretion of dopamine in the brain could subject a person to delusional episodes, which is one symptom of psychosis. Most of the drugs of abuse also release dopamine, exacerbating the effect of cortisol during chronic stress. You may know that hallucination is common to those who are using illicit drugs. This is also one reason why they can commit brutal crimes and murders.

Chapter 4:   Effectively Dealing with Loneliness

Dealing with loneliness is the same as dealing with stress. Loneliness and stress cannot be totally eliminated in a person's system because of the different and numerous stressors that come from the environment. Loneliness cannot be attributed to a single cause alone.

Loneliness is a reaction in response to a stimulus you have received. The exposure to emotional disturbances creates chemical reactions in your body and mind. This will cause impairment in the physiological processes in your body.

Reactions will occur in your body to regain homeostasis that was disturbed by the stimulus. These reactions will not stop until your body has attained balance. But the persistent, continuous triggering of the stimulus can exhaust your body and cause permanent damage.

What are the signs of loneliness?

1. Forgetfulness
2. Feeling of fatigue
3. Low self esteem

4. Poor decision making

5. Irritability

6. Moodiness

7. Preference to be alone

8. Unproductive at work

9. Inability to communicate well

10. Insufficient sleep

11. Indulging in alcohol drinking, smoking and/or using prohibited drugs

How to prevent loneliness

How can you prevent loneliness? Here are simple and doable steps you can start incorporating in your day:

Step #1 - Recognize that you are lonely

Acknowledge your loneliness, but remember that this can happen to anyone. You cannot prevent stressors from coming in because it is from everywhere and can be anything, but you must be alert to identify it.

Step #2 - Analyze why you are lonely

If you know the stressor, then you must know the possible effects in your body. What's the stimulus that prompted you to feel lonely? Recognition of the stimulus and its effects on your body is the best way to cope with its adverse effects on your health. You can readily manage your loneliness when you understand what causes it because you can then avoid these stimuli.

Step #3 - Try to unwind

Go for a walk. Do not focus on what's troubling you. Try to perceive the positive thing about the situation. It's only in appreciating the positive things around you that you can overcome the negative.

Step #4 - Bond with your family

The family is the basic anchor you can hold on to when you feel lonely. Use family therapy as a means to combat loneliness. Connect and spend more quality time with your family members. You can also bond with your friends and co-workers. Engaging in group therapy can be useful, if you don't have a supportive family and friends.

Step #5 - Avoid controlled substances

Loneliness can make you prone to drinking, smoking and using illicit drugs because they can serve as a temporary escape from your loneliness and depression. You must always be alert to this possibility. Think positively and persevere in maintaining an optimistic attitude towards things and events.

Step #6 - Ask a trusted confidant for advice

Confide in a trusted friend with whom you can talk freely and openly. This is what you need most in times like this. You have to accept the fact that you are unable to concentrate and make wise decisions, so it is better to have someone to talk to regarding the things that are troubling you.

Step #7 - Document your progress

When a person is lonely, being forgetful is common. So, take down notes and list your plans for the day. Write down your progress. Did you feel less lonely today or yesterday? What triggered you to become less lonely or lonelier? Through these notes, you can then avoid the stimuli that set off your feelings of loneliness.

Step #8 - Take a breather from your usual activities

Take a leave of absence from work. Take a vacation for several days, a week, or a month to get away from the humdrum of your daily existence. Go someplace where the stimuli are missing and enjoy yourself. Forget all about your worries and anxieties. Forget about the reasons why you feel lonely. Throw all your worries and loneliness in the trash can of your mind and start anew.

Step #9 - Reward yourself

Treat yourself to a full body massage in a classy spa. Get a spanking haircut. Buy a new dress, a pair of jeans or shoes. Eat your favorite ice cream or cake. Exercise and stretch your muscles at the gym. Have a date with your loved one or with someone exciting. Just have fun and that's all. This would be a great time for you to do things you have not done during your working days.

Step #10 - Make yourself happy

No one can make you happy but yourself. Don't think that your happiness is dependent on other people. Happiness is a state of the mind and doesn't depend on how rich, how successful or how intelligent you are. It's a choice that you have to make consciously. Do it for yourself and not for anyone else. This time, you should not expect anything from other people, so that you won't get disappointed in the end.

Step #11 - Seek medical help for prolonged loneliness

It is better to seek medical attention rather than pile up the ill health effects of loneliness in your mind and body.

Be aware that loneliness can lead to depression, suicide and psychological disorders, if you're not able to overcome it. Psychotherapy is of significance in these cases.

There are different types of psychotherapy that could be a great help:

- **Behavioral therapy**
  Behaviorists believe that unwanted behavior can be eliminated and be replaced by a more desired behavior through proper conditioning and new learning.

  This therapy uses positive and negative reinforcement to motivate changes in your behavior; the therapist will help you modify unwanted behavior by exposing you to the stimulus. One good example is in the management of agoraphobia. If your phobia concerns places where you can't escape from, then constant exposure to these kinds of places will eventually allow you to conquer your fear. This should be done with the guidance of a competent therapist.

- **Cognitive therapy**
  Cognitive therapy uses the power and strength of the mind to adapt to a new behavior. Therapists believe that if an individual can change his thoughts, he can also change his behavior.

  The therapist will present the effects of your unwanted behavior and this knowledge of all possible consequences that might result will help you avoid that unwanted behavior. This can help you make informed choices. If the therapy succeeds, you should be choosing the desired behavior and shunning the unwanted actions. This therapy enhances your capability to overcome difficulties and thus, exemplifies your strength in modifying your behavior.

- **Psychodynamic therapy**

  This is a kind of therapy where the patient is being reconciled with his past thoughts, memories and childhood experiences. The therapist analyzes your repressed feelings by asking questions, and then focuses more on your answers. What were your struggles and difficulties that have caused your state of mind? This will give the therapist some insight into the possible cause of your troubles. The therapist will interpret the results.

- **Humanistic therapy**

  This therapy focuses more on what you can achieve in the future, rather than delving and investigating your past. It can encourage you to attain your own maximum potential, promote your personal growth and turn you into a new person. It can inspire you to make rational decisions based on informed choices. You and the therapist will work hand in hand to achieve your self-actualization. Acceptance of yourself as a valuable person is the primary purpose of this therapy.

These are the steps and strategies you can implement to deal with your loneliness. The key aspect to remember is that only you can truly resolve your loneliness. Change can only come from within.

Chapter 5: How to Never Feel Alone Again

Loneliness is one of the superficial phases of depression. Let's face the truth. Let's go deeper into the complexity and causes of loneliness. When you speak about loneliness, most of the time you may think that loneliness will eventually pass; that it is nothing serious and there's nothing to worry about. Well, you're right in some ways, but there's more to it than just feelings.

What if you can't help it?

When loneliness does come from unjustified discrimination and persecution, from the hurt and pain of betrayal from your loved ones, from a failed marriage, from the loss of someone beloved, from human trafficking and cases of rape, how can someone not experience loneliness, trauma, or depression?

There are crimes that are happening in the real world, and sometimes, you become a victim involuntarily. You become utterly lonely when justice is not given to those who need them most; when those with evil interests appear to succeed and rule; when justice is only for those who have money and connections; this can give you a deep sense of loneliness because you know that justice delayed is, in fact, denied.

In this particular case, you must understand that you have the responsibility to do all you can to help resolve the issue. BUT, you cannot carry the weight of the whole world on your shoulders. You have to understand that being helpless in the face of a gigantic responsibility can't be helped. Do the best you can to quit being lonely and depressed. Focus on the positive aspects of things around you instead. Think about the billions of good people who have the same thoughts as you and who are trying their best to help solve the problem too. Start from there and everything will be fine. You can also start healing yourself from within.

Healing will not come from the outside, it stems from within. Many have tried to get healing from outside sources such as, advice from families or friends, reading self-help books or engaging in activities to forget loneliness. Yes, it is true, they are of help, but these methods will only give you temporary relief.

Healing your loneliness must come from inside you. Do you want to know how? The healing process discussed next is one way you can cope with your loneliness.

Questions are intentionally included to help you go through the process successfully. Each step requires you to take time and think before proceeding to the next level.

The Healing Process

- Find a quiet and comfortable place. It is only you who can assess what is quiet and comfortable for you.

- Lie down and close your eyes.

- Take a few minutes to relax and maintain your breathing.

- Now, think of what has happened and what is happening to you right now.

- Are you hurt and in deep pain? Do you feel the utter loneliness engulfing your being? Do you feel alone, beaten-up and depressed?

  You must answer these questions before you can proceed.

  If your answer is no, then you need not continue.

- Think again, what is the most important thing to you? Your answer, most probably, would be your family.

37

- Cling to the thought that your family is still there for you and bask in this knowledge.

- If you have chosen "health", then rejoice in the good news that in spite of everything, you still have your health.

- Whatever you have chosen as the most important thing to you, you should sustain this thought in your mind and be happy that it's still there for you. IT'S NOT THE END OF THE WORLD! Quit being lonely and start being happy for whatever you have, and whoever you are.

Chapter 6: Helpful Tips in Conquering Loneliness

1. **Loneliness is not a number; it's a state of the mind.** Don't equate loneliness with the number of people around you. Being alone doesn't mean you're lonely and vice versa.

2. **Be an optimist.** Acquiring a positive outlook will help you overcome your loneliness. There is always a positive side to any given situation, no matter how bad it seems. Strive to find the positive aspect in everything you encounter - always.

3. **Acquire new hobbies.** Do something you're passionate about. If you don't have an existing hobby, find one and engage in it actively. Useful hobbies can be reading, writing, painting, hiking, playing the piano, photography or sports.

4. **Love yourself.** Loving yourself must be a given. You cannot overcome loneliness if you hate yourself. But how can you love yourself in spite of your imperfections? By learning to appreciate what you have. An example is appreciating your complete set of fingers, your normal nose, your pair of legs, your normal ears, your...there are a lot of things you can love yourself for.

5. **Be less critical of yourself and others.** When you're uptight and critical of yourself and of other people, you will feel lonely most often because no one is perfect. It's a fact that you have to accept. When you learn to accept that each individual has shortcomings and at the same time good traits, then you will feel less lonely.

6. **Find time to socialize.** Although loneliness doesn't mean not having company around you, it may be of helpful to have people you can spend time with, especially during holidays. They can be your family or friends.

7. **Keep a daily account of the events for the day.** Create a logbook where you can write down all that happened to you in a day. Remember to express your feelings and thoughts of what transpired. This can help track your progress in overcoming your loneliness.

8. **Join a support group.** You can do this online or offline. Doing it online is more convenient and quicker. Through your support group, you can share your experiences and learn how others have coped with their own loneliness. You can use an alias to protect your identity if you're not comfortable with the activity.

9. **Get down to the root cause of your loneliness.** You may not know it, but your loneliness can also be due to hormonal problems. Hence, no matter how hard you try to overcome your feeling of loneliness and depression, it will still persist. If you suspect the cause is physiological, schedule a medical check-up and determine whether your endocrine glands are functioning normally.

10. **Desensitize yourself against the stimulus of your loneliness.** When you have found out the cause of your loneliness, try to desensitize yourself to it by exposing yourself repeatedly to this stimulus. If you find that desensitization worsens your loneliness, then take steps to evade the stimulus instead.

11. **Enjoy your moments of aloneness.** Some people don't realize that solitude can elicit happiness. It's during aloneness that you can have the whole world to yourself. You can do the things you have wanted to do and enjoy the thoughts you have wanted to dwell on. Again, let me reiterate this: aloneness is not loneliness.

12. **Improve yourself.** Feeling lonely sometimes stems from lack of self-confidence. You can resolve this issue by improving yourself. Learn new skills and continue your education. No matter what you have attained, you are a unique individual, and no one can ever take your place in this world. It's an amazing fact

that is true, just as no two fingerprints are alike amidst the trillions of people in the world.

Conclusion

Dealing with loneliness is a personal matter. This is due to the fact that you – alone – can overcome your loneliness. No one can do it for you. Keep in mind that loneliness is a state of the mind. Believe and trust in yourself that you can overcome your loneliness. You must learn to love your own company and make the most out your aloneness.

Having a positive frame of mind can also help significantly in resolving your loneliness. This will help make you happy and less critical of yourself and of others. It will also allow you to acquire friends and develop new hobbies. This will eventually ease your feelings of loneliness.

Make yourself happy instead of lonely by following the information provided in this book. They are simple and doable, so you won't have any problem implementing them. Good luck!

Finally, I'd like to thank you for purchasing this book! If you found it helpful, I'd greatly appreciate it if you'd take a moment to leave a review on Amazon. Thank you!

Made in the USA
Lexington, KY
22 July 2016